BEGINNING HISTORY

TUDOR TOWNS

Joanne Jessop

Illustrated by Peter Dennis

Wayland

BEGINNING HISTORY

The Age of Exploration

The American West

Crusaders

Egyptian Farmers

Egyptian Pyramids

Family Life in World War II

Greek Cities

The Gunpowder Plot

Medieval Markets

Norman Castles

Plague and Fire

Roman Cities

Roman Soldiers

Saxon Villages

Tudor Sailors

Tudor Towns

Victorian Children

Victorian Factory Workers

Viking Explorers

Viking Warriors

All words that appear in **bold** are explained in the glossary on page 22.

Series Editor: Deborah Elliott
Book Editor: James Kerr
Designer: Helen White

First published in 1990 by Wayland (Publishers) Limited, 61 Western Road,
Hove, East Sussex BN3 1JD

British Library Cataloguing in Publication Data
Jessop, Joanne
Tudor towns.
1. England. Towns, history
I. Title   II. Series
942.009732

HARDBACK ISBN 1-85210-780-4

PAPERBACK ISBN 0-7502-0528-8

Typeset by Kalligraphic Design Limited, Horley, Surrey.
Printed in Italy by G. Canale & C.S.p.A., Turin.
Bound in Belgium by Casterman, S.A.

CONTENTS

THE TUDOR PERIOD

Ships brought goods in and out of London along the River Thames.

Tudor is the family name of the kings and queens who ruled England from 1485 to 1603. This time in history is known as the Tudor period.

During the Tudor period, England became rich by selling wool and cloth to other countries. Many people moved from the countryside to cities and towns to set up businesses or to look for work.

London was by far the biggest city and the most important centre for trade and business in Tudor England.

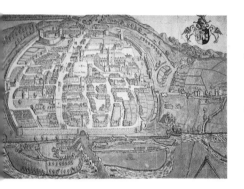

Above *A map of Exeter in 1587.*

THE TOWN STREETS

The streets of Tudor towns were busy and noisy places during the day. Traders and shopkeepers shouted out to attract customers. People spent a lot of time on the streets because their houses were small and dark.

Town streets were filthy and smelly. Dirty water was flung out of windows and rubbish was left to rot on the streets.

At night the streets became quiet. Most people were in their homes by nightfall. There was always the danger of being attacked or robbed in the dark, unlit streets.

Right *A Tudor town house.*

HOUSES

Rich **merchants** had grand town houses built. For the first time, chimneys were added to take smoke from the fireplaces out of the houses.

But even so, the houses of the rich were uncomfortable. They had no indoor toilets, no tap water and not much furniture. The master of the house might have an armchair, but children sat on stools.

A poor family's house was usually one small room with a hole in the wall for a window. They slept on straw with only a blanket to keep themselves warm.

A cutaway illllustration of a wealthy Tudor family's house.

SHOPS

There were all kinds of shops in Tudor towns: baker's, butcher's, candle maker's and shoemaker's. The shopkeeper used the lower room of his house as a workshop, and he and his family lived upstairs. In the

morning, the shutter of the downstairs window was lowered to make a counter, from which goods were sold.

The shopkeeper usually belonged to a **guild.** He employed **apprentices** who worked for seven years learning the skills of the trade. They could then be accepted into the guild and set up their own shops.

Above *This was the sign of a guild.*

Left *An illustration of a shopping scene from the 1500s.*

FAMILY LIFE

The children of poor families worked hard. They had to help their parents or work as servants or apprentices in other households. The sons of rich merchants were sent to school while the daughters stayed at home and learned how to be good housewives. There was little time for children to play.

Below *A house belonging to a wealthy Tudor family.*

In the evenings, the family might play musical instruments and sing for entertainment. But most people went to bed when the sun went down.

SCHOOLS

School for Tudor children meant long hours of hard work, with only short breaks for breakfast and lunch. They went to school six days a week and had few holidays. Only boys attended school during the Tudor period.

The main subjects taught at school were **Latin,** Greek and religion. Students were expected to speak to each other in Latin, not English. They wrote with **quill pens** and had

Right *A painting of a teacher and pupils from the 1500s.*

to learn lessons by heart because there were few books. If a student did not do well at his lessons, the teacher would beat him with a wooden rod.

RELIGION

Religion was an important part of life in Tudor times. Everyone had to go to church on Sunday or else pay a fine. Church bells were rung to call people to church and to let them know when it was time for work and for meals.

During Tudor times there were many disagreements between **Catholics** and **Protestants.** Many people were punished for their religious beliefs; some were even burned at the stake.

Above *Tudor churches often had stained-glass windows like this.*

Left *This is the sort of church you would find in many Tudor towns.*

17

CRIME AND PUNISHMENT

There was a lot of crime in Tudor towns and cities. Many criminals were poor people who could not find work and so became thieves. Criminals were not often caught because there were few policemen. For those who were caught,

punishments were very cruel. Thieves were strangled or hanged. Murderers were hanged, burned or boiled to death. **Traitors** had their heads chopped off. These punishments were carried out in public as a warning to others.

For small crimes, such as cheating a customer, criminals were put in **stocks,** and passers-by would throw rotten food at them.

ENTERTAINMENT

Most people were kept busy at work
or at school during the week, so
Sundays and Church **holy days**
were the times for having fun. People
danced, sang and played games such
as dice, draughts, cards and chess.
Some people enjoyed themselves by

watching bears being set on by dogs. This cruel sport was known as bear-baiting. Cock fights were also popular.

Most townspeople liked to watch plays. The first London **theatres** were built during Tudor times. London had many other exciting entertainments, including a zoo at the Tower of London.

21

GLOSSARY

Apprentices People who work for craftsmen to learn the skills of a craft.

Catholics Members of the Christian Church headed by the Pope in Rome.

Guild An organization of people who practised the same craft.

Holy days Days on which religious festivals were celebrated.

Latin The language spoken by the ancient Romans.

Merchants People who make money by buying and selling goods.

Protestants Christians who are not members of the Roman Catholic Church.

Quill pens Pens made from the hollow stems (the quills) of birds' feathers.

Stocks A wooden frame with holes for a person's feet to be locked into as a punishment.

Theatres Places where people go to watch plays.

Traitors People who went against the king or queen.

BOOKS TO READ

Elizabeth I and Tudor England by Stephen White-Thomson (Wayland, 1984).

Everyday Life in the Sixteenth Century by Haydn Middleton (Macdonald, 1982).

Growing Up in Elizabethan Times by Amanda Clarke (Batsford, 1980).

King Henry VIII by Dorothy Turner (Wayland, 1987).

The Tudors by Tim Pashley (Wayland, 1985).

INDEX

Picture acknowledgements

The publishers would like to thank the following for providing the photographs in this book: C M Dixon 6 (top), 11 (top), 12 (bottom), 17 (top); Michael Holford 6 (bottom), 17 (bottom); Syndication International 14 (bottom); Wayland Picture Library 11 (bottom).